# *Vox Humana*

# *Vox Humana*

E. Alex Pierce

Brick Books

Library and Archives Canada Cataloguing in Publication

Pierce, E. Alex, 1943-
     Vox humana / E. Alex Pierce.

Poems.
ISBN 978-1-926829-71-5

I. Title.

PS8631.I469V69 2011          C811'.6          C2011-904252-5

We acknowledge the Canada Council for the Arts, the Government
of Canada through the Canada Book Fund, and the Ontario Arts
Council for their support of our publishing program.

   Canada Council    Conseil des Arts
                for the Arts      du Canada       Canada

The cover image is a photograph by George Steeves from the series
"The Pictures of Ellen," © George Steeves, Collection of the National
Gallery of Canada.

The author photograph was taken by Les French.

The book is set in Bliss and Minion.

Design and layout by Alan Siu.

Printed and bound by Sunville Printco Inc.

Brick Books
431 Boler Road, Box 20081
London, Ontario  N6K 4G6
www.brickbooks.ca

For my mother, Eileen Lloyd Pierce.

# Contents

*Now I should add that the light here is heartbreakingly beautiful, the marshes green gold, the creek water clear; how there comes a desire simply to merge with it, to lie down, curl one's body into an earth shape, die with the leaves, bend into that lucent sky, become the vagabond, the wanderer, the invisible, the other, the lost child that every child is, the one before becoming, before they made us who we are, the voice that is the under-singing, the one we have forgotten.*

# In the Sand Hills

Down in the dunes is a language place, lost U-vowel of the sound turned round,
guts of the rabbit strewn over ground. Grit of the fir cones, peeled by squirrels.

No one is here. Shadow of a lost imagined pony skin, lichen scab
creeps over the dune ridge. Trees, grown up, grown over, an acre of sand.

Layer of forest floor, tangle of alder – closing the pathways. Tongue
of cold sand, far up inland, a half mile from shore – I want it back.

I want it all clean. I want Mozart in a piano-echoed room, scales in thirds.
I want my mother making shapes of everything, poems in thin air.

My father singing hymns in the car all the way from Sable River
to Liverpool – Hunts Point, Summerville, and Port Mouton.

I want to be always in that car when we slow down for the turn
at Robertsons Lake – that big rock ledge with *the lemonade springs*

*where the bluebird sings in the Big Rock Candy Mountain.* I want to be
in that clear, sweet space. I want to write my poems then,

grow up again, breathe in that clean, light air. I want to have
my babies then, take them to the Sand Hills, stay

in that sheltered place. I want my clear syllables to drop
on that sand. I want the rain to pelt down our bareback skins

as we ride those pretend ponies, my sister and I,
over the high, white dunes.

I want to speak the sounds I was born to speak –
be the music that played me, safe in that car

as we rolled down the clay-backed road that followed the river
down the flat salt marsh to the edge of the grandmothers' country.

I want not to have lost what I am looking for now. My sounds
are down there, back in those dunes, down at the cold green edge

where we slid down the hot white sand into the cool
damp grey, where roots began and alder intersected,

hid the trails that only rabbits crossed – the place
the tangle started. I want to lie back there
until the words form in my mouth
out of my land and my ground,

my crying places – my self, simple.
Not even happiness.

A bark, a yell, an arc of singing –
a breath. A sound –

is it over – all that over?

Is that where my child, daughter, would have gone –
she too, over?

*This is so bare –*

bare as a bone –

a bone of childhood.

If you could find your own small bone.

ζ

## Boat

The water went by in deep swirling spirals from the oars. The boat passed over the channel, over the eel grass feathering and quickening. It was no good trying to be good, there was no good. And if I don't write it down it will not be written down. It will be lost in the fighting and taking and misery and hatefulness that surrounds us and eats us from childhood and sorrow.

There will be no more voice of the grandfather, the father, calling the channel, knowing its name. Salt sea water entering the river. Opening its way in from the ocean, when the sea was mystery and clean, larger than us, plain.

Because we are not ourselves – ourselves in the boat, moving on the water in perfect peace. We are late for supper, and there is no one home.

## Eternal Lines

My mother spouted lines as if they were
her own: "I could compare thee," she might say.
*Shall I compare thee to a summer's day?*
The poem's truth came later, here, or there,
she'd grafted life to art – *the darling buds
of May* were mine, *his gold complexion dimm'd*,
my father's secret way. *The eye of heaven*
shined on us – and her, until the stroke
that found her vein and played its course
took all her words away. My love for her
was locked inside the poem then – but now
I read to her, and she responds to sound
without the sense, receives the lines she gave:
conceit of childhood – all at once unmade.

# Last Summer in the Old Craig House

Musk melon moth skirt, with those skin-like petals that come in pink and white.
Mauve pink, for musk, our mother, that summer our brother was born.

Gold-spun hair on the gun-metal green lilacs, put there to help the fairies build
their houses. And fairy rings she found in the mossy woods. She was certain of it.

We were two lost princesses travelling with her in her last bid for freedom
while she still ran wild in the meadows and woods-roads,

traipsing us down through the salt marsh to sit on Craig's Beach
and have royal cups of tea, red Kool-Aid that ran in streams

down our white shirts. It was our last summer in that house,
the end of our reign – he came in August, late August.

They put a Union Jack out on the clothesline up the road.
To give birth – to a son.

Lying in that brass iron bed –
now, she was Queen.

## A girl awake

                          in the ell-chamber, night light
only a moon, fear in every limb. Low voices
in the kitchen downstairs, and cats with kittens
kneading under the small back porch.

                          Always some hidden thing
keeping its life going by stealth, in mouthfuls. Water
in the near-empty jam jars, sluicing out the last
sweetness for a glass of summer lemonade. What a waste,
my father said when I followed him out to the furtherest rock
over the ocean. You should have been a boy. More energy
than you know what to do with. *We should harness
the sea.*

What was I? Some wild god, to steal his chariot
out of the waves and haul the familiar sun
across a mackerel sky? Not the boy.
*Because I am the girl.*

Can they see me? My ruched white bathing suit
with silver threads. Was I pretty?
Hair tied up in strips of rags.

In the breakers, I would keep up with him until the water
rose over my head. His bare back, ahead of me. My arms,
my legs, not knowing what I was.

# Ice Mother

Pack ice in spring when the river moves,
shoves blocks up on shore with eel grass frozen
underneath – black streaks inside, like your hair
flown out and coming after me. Ice,
half-worn, half-melted, some of the pieces
higher than my head. I used to feel so safe
like this, inside your temporary shelter.

How fast you used to come and go –

your teeth worn down from grinding,
the force that took you in and out from us,
all quiet now.
                        Ice in chunks, like barges –
I never dared to stand on one and ride
across the river.

                        As if my father
were your saviour, you call out to him,
give him blind love's dumb attention.
*Obedience,* I think, when my compliance
bends to yours, *paid passage in the war
that binds you two.*
                        One side of you
capitulated when you couldn't bear him,
old, and sick, and frightened – now
he cares for you.

                        Do you remember
how you read us *Mary, Queen of Scots,*
*A Tale of Two Cities* – "It is a far, far
better thing …"

But we wanted to know
what it felt like – to lay your head down
on the block, just to wait there,

fresh, and cool, and silent.

# Archduke Trio

Rain, rain, downpour. There is no one in this town who understands her –
alone in the basement room of the house on Zwicker Ave. The cold tile,
twin beds for her and her sister, single beds made from bunks – short, small,

narrow. Hers lies along the wall – from here she can reach the levered window.
Rain floods in tongues down the trunks of the ash trees. Autumn rain in spring,
washes of cold when the soft rain should be coming. In the corner, little

grey box, her phonograph. The arm swings across, needle touches the groove.
Piano – opening bars of the *Archduke Trio*, Beethoven. The records come
in cardboard sleeves, Heritage Recordings of the classics. Her mother

sends away for them. Music in two voices – violin, violoncello. Third voice, piano,
hers. The strings call to the piano. Heart leaps like the white-tailed deer, up, over,
flying, lands, runs – up and down, scales ascending, merging. Music

will not render into words. Beethoven speaks to her – not to her directly, speaks
through the strings – heart, what else but throbbing. Pulse beats in a temple, little
blue vein. Great carotid artery, washes of blood, sobbing held back. He stops.

Piano takes his theme – she will play this. Cello meets piano, growls
into the lower registers, lifts, like water, until the hammered sounds float, surrender
their weight to the greater force. She presses against the cold

wall of the basement, reaches up for the window frame –
in the third movement he takes her to his heaven. No one in the house.
Night, spring night. Piano arcs above the pulsing strings – he takes her

with his architecture, raises a scaffolding up to the dome. Not
quickly – he has time. And now the caress along all her body.
*Andante cantabile ma però con moto.* This blunt, fierce man –

this *man* – speaks a longing that crystallizes hers. It is his not-having
that speaks into her – his ache that stretches her, muscle
from bone, naked heart. Fifteen, and her lover (her mother

says she is too young for boys) – the sound, the rain, the liquid air –
presses her, tongue onto shoulder, mouth onto mouth. She never goes
straight to the slow movement, though she wants it more
than anything – *Allegro moderato, Scherzo (Allegro)* – waits for him.

# Palm Mother

Her hand, flat smooth, her fingers curved up a little from the palm
– palm tree, Palm Sunday, Florida and escape, clattering fronds in
the sea wind. Escape – something else, somewhere else. Her hand,
flat, right over mine, just enough holding to hold me there, in the
church, tongue and groove in the pews, on the walls, hymn-singing,
holding it *holy holy* in, all the tremor in her, the edge of her stroke, his
Parkinson's not quite started, all of it trembling. *Waiting to happen,*
she said.

The way she would hold her fingers like that. The time she cut herself
on the tuna can lid, her hand held out and saying it was our fault.
Something soft in the way the blood streamed.

In the Metropolitan Museum, *Mummy of Artemidora, Daughter of
Harpokras.* The inscription: *...died untimely, aged 27. Farewell.* That
same hand, flat along the mummy case, fingers identical, the left
hand. Lying as if in her bed. At the foot of the case, Anubis, god of the
underworld *bearing the disk of the moon.*

I keep her photo from Florida glued to the fly-leaf of a book. Her face,
half hopeful, sunglasses pushed back on her head. She's standing in
the entryway, palms outside along the beach. Something beating at
her temple. Him calling her from inside. *Not letting anybody out.*

# Reading Shakespeare

She looks under the pillow. She cannot find her words. She keeps
a little list. How did she write that out? A list of pencilled cursives
sketched on scraps of foolscap paper, irregular verbs – something
she'd give her high-school students. How *lie* becomes *lay, write*
becomes *wrote* – *smite, smote.* "I lay in the bed all day. I would like
to write you, but my pen would not obey me, so – " She stops.

He says, *Devouring time.* He says, *Let us not*
*to the marriage.* Says, *Thou art more lovely.* She sighs.
The list goes back under the pillow.

She cannot not remember. She cannot read the words,
small *and's* and *the's* and *now's* and *after's* – linkages
she cannot make. *Out damned spot* – there is no perfume
to sweeten or to make forget. Sometimes, after reading,
I put my head down on her chest, and rest there
on the flannel nightgown. There is no end to this.

## Aunt Edna

Cursive, that scribing arm – it has something to tell.
Her arm has chosen me. The body cannot wait.
The arm swings, back, forth, repetitive
on the sheets. I ought to take her hand.
I want to want to. The elbow bends
to shield her eyes – iron blue, brown rims
with no centre and no light. Am I there?

The arm, unhinged, derails the hand, the hand
reminds the face – so old. She shifts, voluptuary,
riming into sleep. I see her, naked, turning
to a lover, her hair is long and flowing down,
caught in the tortoise shell of combs. She winds,

old serpent, in her bed. She
lets me see her.

# Because to the majesty

of the illness, the place
between retreat and recovery, came the return
of the voice, not trumpeting, like that, not
barely heard in the scooping up of everyday,
just before, just after, the relief unto death,
but telling itself as we had, in our cribs
in our nightgowns (all girls, all telling)
in the story voice that comes on, just under.

*And to you is the glory the everlasting, the world
going on without you, amen* – because, unwritten,
we had still to tell it, even to air, become air
to say, *This ancient un-selfing of me joined to you,
this is the heart's tale, reminding return, nothing
between us – will part us – or save us.*

## Travelling with My Mother

She looks out from a great distance as if she were riding a boat.
*I can't go that way,* she says. She turns from the window,
away from her left side, which follows her. *You know,* she says.
Pale blue walls. At the top of the white chenille bed cover,
a yellow flower. Down in the bed, floating, see. *See something
gone.* Flower comes back – light on that side.
Legs inside and cover over. *Feet stay out.*
Now I pull the top cover back – *I found it,* she says,
and strokes the yellow flower.


She rides the boat a long way. I speak to her. She says,
*Yes, yes.* The bed looks small and far – so long
to slide down. Blue and soft, light and not.
Tied back, so white. *Light in.* I say I know. As long
as it is wide, her room. Iron and stubborn
the bed. Settle under – she wraps her head up,
holds the sheet up to her nose. *Listen, listen.* Breathe.
*It's cold.* Slide up. The distance from her bed to the door
is the distance of mountains. We go it together.

## Vox humana

The thing which has no voice,
refuses to speak, is a thing
flayed and pitiless. It will
survive, it will swim

through the passages and corridors
of its undertaking –
it will name itself vagrant,
subordinate, unfledged, vestigial,

faultless, sweet – until it strike
by accident or design, a surface
abrasive, unreflective,
which does not require beauty.

Feeling the probe of its fish-nudge,
floating in a current at last
recognizable, it will sing to itself,
I am, I am

misshapen, unlovely, unadorned,
unknowable –
disjunctive, implacable, illicit,
unreasonable –

feral, wily,
free.

## No Address

I want to come into a room,
for you to be there, to stand quietly
beside me while I sit in the chair.
I want you to stand close.

I can feel you there.

I want you to put your hand on my face –
now I can speak. In this bare room
what can come of me? Your letter
lies in my lap. What can be said?

Nothing will come of me.

I will feel you standing there. I will feel my face
moving out of itself. I will hear the ice melting
on the roof. I will give away all that is left,
remnant and scrap – say nothing.

Nothing will speak.

# Their Boy

There are four of them up on that sun-struck hill:
two in grieving agony for their dead son, two
walking to comfort them – walking into the light,
holding on to him all the long afternoon, holding
his presence, this absence of his presence, which is
the light itself, the snow's blindness, the breathing glare.

She can feel him, his mother – and the boy's father knows
he must keep walking to hold her holding of him. It's like walking
with her pregnant, all those Sundays, seeing her big and round
and stretched. Imagining their boy coming towards them,
in through their twined bodies, coming in to them.

They go between the trees, part from one another, like
shades themselves, pulling his image down to them. Snow
under foot, wet tree trunks, raw wind, snapped branches.
They're holding it open, an unfurled, sunlit day –
*take an arm, take my eye* – wanting to bargain.

Their coats are unbuttoned. Friends slip an arm
through an arm. They pace on. It's like a search,
the body already found. Pacing. With him still close.
Still in them, between them. There's a voice on the wind
they can't hear anymore. *Mum, Dad.* Figures, pacing.

Giving him up.

## Driving Back

I have been in the far country, place of the dead.
Driving back, under the sky's wide shoulders, the sky reaching
out and out the only protection – spent grasses
of my mind's uncollected thoughts, bits, twigs, hopes
for a future, random scraps and wild twinings, all woven now, shaped
and stuck down with mud, a nest for the arrival of grief –
I know exactly where you are.

Will I give birth to you? See with your eyes for this little time?
How long will I hold down the wild howl, this long breath that draws
in but will not out.
                        I can keep this place just a few hours more,
just the length I must drive – away from you, away from the everywhere
you are now. Try to keep this intensity of your clear eyes seeing.
Through me.

## Slow Music

A slow music starts. You know it – it's old,
older than you. This music cuts a line,
shoulder to hip, crossing the heart – wait
for it to deepen on its fateful way.

It passes through you, and when you turn
to it, turn in, not towards, take this in
to the part of you that calls itself home –
you're already changed, cannot

go back. Listen, you're not unusual,
unrealistic, even unreliable. Until
this morning, you were unloved, un-
touchable, untouched. So music starts,

all of it, all for you. Marked now, spoken for,
even though you don't believe it – sung.

# The Snakes Transform in the Woodpile

Even the eyes moult, growing larger
under the skin that covers them – a skin
that thin, purely transparent, holding them
intact, so they can do their work. What do they see
at the moment of moulting? The snake
that was, the snake that will become – split,
blind, as the lost world memorizes itself, still
present in the cells that lift off,
as light as paper?

                The final eye
looks inward, sighting back along the spinal tube,
the aperture quiescent, until a rippling signal
prompts the inverse motion, peeling
then from now – and ends
the doubled world,

             which must be
what her eyes see, as she lies, old woman
in her hospital bed, old aunt staring out.

             Watching her sleep,
three nights now – an arm got loose,
inscribed the air, drew the hand
along her shoulder, round the hairline
then her breast all shrunken in, but curved
the way that hand was touching it.

                              She
dropped her head towards her shoulder, waited
for the arm, then moved her restless mouth
against its skin – as if
she wanted to caress, encourage
what was hers,
what was passing away.

They looked like cobwebs, the skins in the woodpile.
They looked like strips of cloth, old nylons
in a bureau drawer – between the lengths
of spruce-wood piled up for winter.  This
was their sequestered place.

Like sticks, the snakes must have lain there afterwards.
Like lovers, startled, still too new to move –

and then   their eyes   would open.

# Common Loons

We are in the feather bed, thirteen, so close
our nightgowns touch. You have bangs cut
straight across. Downstairs we danced from
the moment the Victrola needle pricked. June roses
from the field outside in every glass tumbler
we could find. The parlour in this abandoned house
contains our crazy dancing. There's a dusty rug,
Aunt Mabel's choice, flowers in swirls, and ball fringe
on the horsehair furniture. It is almost pain, waiting
for the needle to come down. Then the rough scratching
while it searches for the groove. As we go round, waltzing
in each other's unaccustomed arms, *The Charge of the Light
Brigade* reverses and swings in its frame on the wall.

Their bayonets are ready. Their tall hats and bright braid
look almost foolish on that battleground. Lined up,
lined up. And death will come. In bed, we hear the
loons, late, over Johnson's Pond. Their night-hoots
follow the racoon's squeal, the rats' rustling. We are
not afraid. Something deep, sweet, and impossible
drifts toward the centre of the bed. The feathers
drown us. The common loon's uncommon laughter
trills and spirals down our spines. *Cruising down the river*
sings the Victrola. But we are past that now, pulled
into the lake's depth, diving with the loons, necks stretched,
mouths open, eardrums closed. Twenty, thirty years from now
you will come to my door with your ancient father and give me
a rose slip you have dug up from that field.

## Vox animalia

A piece of alder. Tap, tap, tap – back of the jackknife,
and the bark-skin comes off. Slides, sap smoothing.
Then the cut, just the angle needed for sound.

Length of your index finger, whistle. Little pipe.
So the porcupine – windpipe, larynx tipped back
to make those human sounds. Have you heard them?

Nighttime in the spruce boughs. Insistent cries.
And if you could see their feet, you would never
kill one. Feet like a human baby's feet. Voice

calling out on a breath that makes love, mates –
all night in the spruce trees. Something between
a holler and a grunt, a voice that imitates our young,

holds a note and sobs on it, boughs creaking, rubbing –
and then a little cough. Alone, in the tent we lie
and listen. No one wants a porcupine – quills

filled with air. Slow moving, forepaws like a beaver's.
Insatiable – all night eating apple boughs.
All night loving, quills softened. They sound like us,

another *vox humana*, like the organ pipe, relic
in the parlour. Pump organ, stops labelled
*vox, vox, vox* – tremolo, bellows filling air.

Take this creature into your throat pipe. Gristle,
heft, and hide. Rasp, slide the whistle – the alder
cuts its throat to speak its sound.

# Shelter

We were there in that dark with the bleat
and the crying around us. I could still hear you,
in that other language, speaking to them, to the lambs.

I stood still and wouldn't move,
fearful to go and fearful to stay,
the storm's voice coming from without,
the animals' voice, within.

And I knew them, that they were safe now.

Then the luxury of the lambs came down,
and you were there where you wished to be,
upon me, rippling out and outer
with a sound of wind over wind and rain over rain,
of wool over wool and flesh over flesh,
the sound of a sound folding into itself,
until my bones were glad to be that frame
over which my skin, like a tent, had stretched itself.

## Desdemona

Once I prayed to him, and the sweet, killing
concert of his voice rolling under me,
his eyelids closing, both, so he'd not see me,
fleeing what we knew ourselves to be –
flesh of pears, cobs, dogs. Spiderlings,
alert to the bramble taste on our tongues.

His fingers' touch – I craved him – now a rising bruise
edged brownish, foolish, ripe. His back the earth,
and I the sky reversed – he was my lord,
and not my love, my lord, all wound
and through me.  How press away desiring –
caught, caught – entangled in these strands.

*Oh, my lord,* I said. *My lord, what wilt thou?*
Thou. You, me. *I –*

When I said *I,* I lost him. He –
offering the halved, tinged pear
against my mouth.

# My Jerusalem

For you I will live my own corruption.
I will ride my own evil
up to the gates of hell.

I will bring an army,
which I will destroy
outside your walls.

You, my city,
my surrender –
I do not care

how many whores have loved you,
only be there, shining,
when I come.

## You wrote to me

                     – you said I blew through town
like an effervescent veil. Again, I thought, there it is again,
the waft of silk between us. I used to be so glad to see you –
just to borrow some of your life so I could make up mine.
To have a place, to belong –
and not like fog, to everyone.

## Madonna of the Pinks

*This is the title of a painting by Raphael (1483-1520)*
*commissioned c.1506 for Maddalena degli Oddi of Perugia to*
*take with her to the convent where she intended to seek refuge*
*following her refusal of a proposed marriage.*

Ring of metal, Saturn's halo,
carries this restraint –
bride's wish place,
unacknowledged, sequestering.

It is the liquid quality of the veil,
a skim of rippling light
that strikes to the heart
of the matter – what is
the matter? Here –
the *materia*, flame,
floats about her head. She is
with child, of course, for
all who are without –

*Holy mother, girl thing, perfection's*
*lips have brushed you, painted*
*out what blushed when you,*
*impossibly, became.*

≈

Mistress, who sings now,
holds the plum blossom to her cheek,
pretends indifference – and is,
sick of heart, already packing.
What will she need
for her unrequited life?

The image floats before her,
inviolate. Accompaniment, perhaps.
Perhaps nothing. A pure space,

days of contemplation,
a feeling of self,
no other.

The child reaches for the petals,
beams, suckles, grows fat.

# Solstice

It is the eye
of winter, this slit
that lets in light.

Stones crack and breastplates
fall when fire speaks.

A shuddering nor'easter pastes
snow on every ledge, and steam's
recurring breath uncoils
from the sea. What is it

to say that light has entered earth? The dead
of winter rise with open mouths, mock
soft limbs of early spring. But listen,

here's what's true. She touched,
I opened.

# Reading You

Cold comfort (*How cold my toes, tiddely-pom...*)
to read you when I'd rather have you –
to have you, God forbid, then leave you.
Lying here, alone (*And nobody knows*),
surprised by love –  that little time, sweet
poised measure, one tablespoon of, say it,
*nectar*, taken by a hummingbird in sips –
for us, one gulp of sudden joy.

Reading you, alarmed at every turn you take
each time you pass along my nerve ends'
reckoned memory of things we've never done,
I want to shout, *Stop writing over all the moments,
undo this cursor, cursed time's sharp quill –
oh, dance with me, stand still.* This hold
you hold me in should never end – it never will.

# The Returning

How can I ask if you will come back? You will
not come back. There cannot be return
from the gates, the palaces of a place not earth
where they say you have gone. Bring me your shirt,
a necktie, a pair of your socks, any thing.
Bring a cup you've drunk from, a spoon
you've put in your mouth. I will cry out from happiness,
I will stop all this. I will, like the shutter's eye, open
for my slice of eternity. I forgot – for a moment
I thought you might have come into the room.

I cannot bear to stop. When I stop you are not here,
you are everywhere – at once – in me,
outside of me. And not. What can you have become?
Some winged creature, some transformation
of your simple, earthly self? There is nothing
I believe in, see, or sense. I walk over
to a window, I sit down in a chair. I stare
past that hollow in the ground –
and the sound I hear, intangible, not even
the echo of your voice.

If you are changed now, become one of them,
I know your dear, plain self will not return.
There is no safe return. Today, a girl is swimming
off the coast, swept overboard. The heart
stops for her – *keep on, keep on.* How can she
keep on? How alone is the body – out there?
Oh, let you never be alone. Let one of us hold you
constantly, in this strange ether that is your realm
no longer. Each of us treading,
treading, supporting you

with our tired arms. Until one day we
just let go, either standing, quiet,
at the cave of light that keeps the entrance
to this place we live, or marking your place
again and again, until no marker stands. We will
wear out with understanding – even breath
wears out.

# Ophelia's Book

*Elsinore, winter:*
Bronchitis again. A month of rain. Last night Gerutha came to sit with me.
I saw her coming down the passage – Nurse had left the door ajar. Her hair
unloosed, she said she couldn't sleep and came to see if I was wakened too.
She stayed and read to me.

*Mid-March:*
The rain is constant, caressing, as nothing else is. I saw him this morning.
He never stops now, illness the excuse. Still a fever, the cough. Rain.

*March, night:*
Gerutha questions me. I tell her Amleth sends me letters, nothing more.

*Spring:*
A thin frost. Walked outside this morning. And the lungs, almost clear.
Such sweet relief.

There are few secrets now. Himself, I think he has forgotten mid-summer.
(Oh my love – every breath goes out of my body when I think of that. An
ebony hand, a balustrade, the viol's curling head, your sweet weight. It will
not do to write this down.)

*April:*
False spring. Gerutha restless. If my light burns at night she will come in.

*May:*
Laertes writes from Paris. *Farouche,* he calls me, *little sister.* I am just so –
half wild, though not that fearful. I went up in the orchard where the King
likes to go and hid myself. I found a piece of rotting alder someone had cut
and left lying in the grass. When it is wet the colour glows blue green. I
know of dyes made from lichens, but this gives more pleasure than those
pale greens.

It is the colour of Amleth's eye.

*May, month's end:*
He came to me. His cloak felt rough. So black.

I found a tri-blossomed flower, red-veined with white petals.
It has a star-shaped heart, almost blue.

Amleth leaves for Wittenberg next month

He promises to write this time, though not in German.
(I keep his likeness in a locket.)

*August:*
My tutor in the morning, then hours to myself. I like to climb up high
on the rocks. When Gerutha admonishes me, I wait until she goes out
on one of her retreats. Tonight she was late and the King in a temper.

I love the willow at the brook. I can cross now, my balance
nearly perfect.

*Mid-September:*
Amleth writes. I have every letter saved. Something
has changed in me. When the willow calls, I go and lie there.

The sound of the water is like wind through pipes.


*October:*
Gerutha, riding out. Only two with her –
no one sees me in the yellow leaves.

When I tire of crossing, I hang from the branches.
It takes all my strength to pull me back up.


*Hallow's Eve:*
White frost. Bright moon.
I think he has forgotten.


*Mid-Winter:*
It is all dark now. His cloak he put
around me – and we lay down. Then he asked
me. Told.

His cloak all black. Inside
my mouth. And I –


*First January:*
The sea, close in, is frozen now.
We will have no letters until spring, unless by land.

*March:*

Black, he was so black. And I
could not stop near him. He
took, cut up my dress. Bars
of iron stayed me. Wasps
undressed me, laid me
down. It was a bramble thorn
that punctured every wound –
and he would speak
incessant. I took his arm's rough
weight. He would not
stay. Against me.

# Penthesilea's Horse

*Penthesilea, Queen of the Amazons, led the Trojan army
into battle to avenge the death of Hector, Priam's son and
Andromache's husband. During the battle with the Greek
forces, Penthesilea met in hand-to-hand combat with Achilles,
slayer of Hector.*

I knew by morning this was our last day. She knew too
in the way humans know things – they watch us for signs.
I longed for her each time she went away. No one
could ride me like her – I wanted her legs
around me. This was the first time she dressed me
for battle, and I was nervous.

                         When Achilles
saw her, he rode in close – I could smell old hay barns
and rotting mint. I saw in his face how he wanted her,
the boy in her and the woman too. The sweat ran
from his arms. She went straight for him –
for Andromache she did this.

                    She breathed into my neck,
our swiftness carried the wind, her hands
pushed under the blades of my shoulders.

                  Three times we pulled in close, made feint
of striking. He fell half sideways, jabbing at nothing,
I saw his big arm, sweat on each hair. She pulled off her helmet
so her hair streamed out – I saw the look in his eyes.

It should all stop there. They should stay there.
In the memory of horses that is just how they are.

                  But he let us close in,
then held back the blow. She struck, he fell –

she moved in.

Then his weight came on top of us, he grappled
in her arms.

           She whispered, *Run Shinkela* –
I felt her breath go. He had her. I rolled forward,
I wanted to crush him. But she grabbed for my mane –
then his sword split the joint of her elbow. When she fell,
her eyes went away from me. I raised up to kill him,
and saw her between us. He spoiled her then
without holding back.

           When he had finished,
he lifted her up. I saw how Achilles was shocked
not to have her.
           This was Penthesilea.
She belonged to no one.

# Cio-Cio San Arrives at Your Door

*Cio-Cio San, called Butterfly, is the heroine of Puccini's opera, Madama Butterfly.*

She seems to cross the lawn between the apple trees,
hardly appears. Her voice clings like the tensile webs
the tent caterpillars hung between the boughs. Her cry
could be the heron's – if the heron sang. The osprey's –
if the osprey turned against itself. The voice sings outside
its fragile body. Porcelain, strung in ligatures of steel. See,
she has spun the trees together. In her wake, peony
blossoms let go their petals in handfuls, black ants
descending among the creamy layers. Each skin-soft
whorl conceals a blush, stain of pink, all the stems
blood-red. Three knocks, she is at the door.

Where can she go in this house? She will mount
the staircase, unsheathe her sword in the north-east
bedroom, climb onto your bed's white cover. Kneel.

Cio-Cio San lifts her arm. Her satin sleeve, the inner
garments lift, and fall again –
                                    her aria will inhabit
your ceilings and your walls. That sound will mourn
against the chambered spaces that open
behind your lath and plaster walls.

                        How would Cio-Cio San live
in such a vacant place? How could she come this far, alone, still
looking for Pinkerton's ship, her spirit drawn up over a cold sea
as she sweeps across the Atlantic, blown off-course
from the Straits of Japan? Butterfly's

wings are strong, she rides the updrafts
of air currents, floats beyond the reach
of any human heart. You have let her in.
Listen. That voice has already altered you.

This winged creature has come, not to pin herself, not even
beg her freedom, press against your faulted glass. She
expects the contract to be honoured. The question
sits, now, in the crevice of your heart.

Change. Change everything. Give up
your quiet places, polished surfaces,
protected hours. Her sword has come for you.

# Athena's Hand on Cassandra's Shoulder

*The title is taken from the label on a stone fragment in the*
*National Archaeological Museum in Athens. Cassandra,*
*princess of Troy, was given the power of prophesy, but cursed*
*never to be believed. Athena, although she fought on the*
*side of the Greeks, was sacred to the Trojans.*

We have only this – the shoulder, and the hand.
Museum fragment, a piece of sculpted stone, four
fingers braced across the scapular blade,
right thumb pressed against the anterior ridge,
Athena's hand on Cassandra's shoulder,
the stubborn torso wrenched away – or can it hold?
If they could stop there, as the gesture stops,
sustaining wisdom's grasp on terror's truth,
would her constricted, tired, smoke-strained throat
released from prophecy make lucid sound
and learn to sing? Would they continue
their protracted dance? If we could stop there,
feel the cool hand drop, the burning vision stilled
and all the towers gone – would we believe her then?

# Hendrick Goltzius' Hand

*Hendrick Goltzius, Dutch Master engraver and painter*
*(1558 - 1617) fell, at the age of one, into the kitchen fire,*
*badly damaging his right hand. Goltzius' drawing of his own*
*disfigured hand (1588) reveals both the extent of the damage*
*and his artist's skill in rendering it.*

And did his mother make that little sound,
her baby's hand stretched out to stop his fall?
She'd reached to snatch him, hold the fire back –
the molten hand, clutched round a coal, refused.
Its flesh insisted – the claw, remaining, grew:
veins laced pathways, sinews scraped and clung,
entwined across the forming bones. It made
an other thing. This strange topography
became the drawer's hand – a channel
for the eye. The sculpted thing could neither
close nor open – and all sensation flowed
into the pen – its nerves refashioned sight.
Perfection brought about by tempering,
the ruined hand annealed in figured light.

## Ophelia's Portrait

*And, with his other hand thus o'er his brow,*
*he falls to such perusal of my face*
*as he would draw it.*

Shakespeare, *Hamlet* II, i.

If such a drawing lives – how does it look?
What shadow lies along my brow so dark
even he can see it? All the water of his being
poured into my eyes, and from them
maddened flowers falling everywhere.
Oh, stop. I want my life. My heart, my soul,
my limbs, my secret's self – all given, all
held back, still nothing felt? I will not give
my life. I'll turn him out of doors, and flee
into the mountains of my mind. There is
another country – even death, a nunnery – No!
This portrait's empty, finished, perfect, lost.
Escape – there's nothing here but misery's cost.

# Anastasia's Soldier

                                  Now she was staring at him.
The men – the old father, the uncles – lay on the dirt floor.
But the girls, they were swirling around. The shot,
meant for birds, should have scattered and killed them
by now. Bodies, blood, weights to be moved. Orders
and shouting, everything over quickly. Above him,
she smiled – the pellets seemed to fall away.
Perhaps she couldn't feel the pain, only startle
and shock. As she whirled past, he caught her –
something that glinted showed through her white dress.
Then came the red, but only in trickles. Her hands flew up,
the sleeves transparent – she had reached for him.
The stories were true, these Romanovs were immortal, after all.
(His comrades out-mastered, what a relief!) If not the Tsar,
that heap on the floor, then the daughters. He
would be the chosen, betrothed to the princess,
he would save her – as now she slips down his arms.

He opens the dress, finds her corsets made of canvas and stays
impregnated with diamonds. The bits of glass pour out
into his hands – her face rests against his. The eyes stop.

Someone else carries her to the cart.

# Sestina on Six Words from Frances Itani's *Deafening*

The child sits in the wind – deafening.
Hearing nothing, she waits for the trees to be still,
holding her centre. She watches the movement of vines.
Safe in the hideout, she guards while her brothers play war.
In the afternoon light, her grandmother brushes the gold-red hair.
When she closes her eyes, she forgets the betrayal of ears.

The scarlet fever has taken her hearing, her ear.
Quiet in the night, the dark of the bedroom deafening,
she reaches for Grandmother, safe in the coils of her hair.
Holding her breath, she waits for the house to be still.
She cannot untangle her childhood fears of their wars.
In the morning her parents attend to the vines.

Outside, the leaves darkening, lime green on their vines.
*He wanted to tell her* – this twining of leaves – in her ear.
The distance between them is private and deadly as war,
this explosion inside him – her arrival – this deafening,
rippling sound. He waits, bound for the time she is still.
He is caught in the beacon, stung by the blaze of her hair.

When they marry, he sleeps in the coils, in the fires of that hair.
They fall on the bed in a ripple and tangle of vines.
In the love that contains them she reaches him, still,
as she catches his words through her fingers, her ears.
He is tuned to her notes, she is safe. Now the deafening
news – the walk to the station. Everyone goes to war.

He is trained as a medic. Her beloved must go. This is war.
He carries the wounded. Rows of beds, broken boys, the lock of red hair.
His heart will explode – lungs explode. Loss is deafening.
They crawl through the mud, limbs, ropes – arms and legs like vines.

*The bearers set down their stretchers.* A boy loses an ear.
They go over the top. *Sounds are worse in the dark.* Death is still.

The letters, the lists. Wounded, missing, POW – heart, be still.
*Soon there will be no one left.* All gone. Little brother, too. War.
Men coming back. This cousin – face shot off, his ear.
The fever, Grandmother nursing her, and the beautiful hair,
gone. *The wind howls, but not the leaves.* Not the vines.
The sight of it – war, the dead, the bloody ugliness. Deafening.

Then it is over. There is only the waiting – deafening, still.
The war, the fever, Grandmother dead. And love returning, like vines,
she to him, he to her – and the glorious hair, his heart, her ear.

## *Ich habe genug*: It Is Enough

It is never enough, what the longing dictates,
smells, sings, and whispers inside the mind. Take this –

*I might have written you, but the sediment was so thin*
*it could not hold ink, nor become paper.*

What is laid down, what lies there, under pressure
becoming rock, waiting, under pressure, to outlive time.

The place we crossed just before noon, on the climb, unnerved me.
There were rocks leaning in on one another like a house or a cave.
Tilted, with openings that made spaces like rooms. At one side and
high up was that mountain shaped like a fortress, just that and the sky.
Out before me and behind me were peaks and vistas, one behind the
other, all separately formed, all folding into mystery. The wind came
so hard down the pass that I wanted to stop, if only for a few moments
inside that rock shelter. But even there the wind came so bold through
the openings that I only entered and came right back out. And I said to
myself, "This is distance. Look at this, look at what distance is made of."

*Even now, I look at these pages, measuring the difference*
*in the width of the pencil marks – yours, and mine.*

I was thinking how far it will be. This is not a phone call or a plane ride.
This is monstrous, impassable, open only a few days in the summer
each year. You could never walk it or even carry it all in your mind.

The other side said, "Look. This is also what links you. The rock layers
join one another under the earth's crust."

"Yes. I see that, too – and it is not of any human size."

Later, I sat down to rest while the others went on up ahead. My T-shirt and undershirt were soaked from the two-hour climb. I noticed the cold only from sitting so long after lunch. I felt safe there, alone on the springy ground cover beside the path. But when I stripped off my wet clothes to change, I saw how unprotected my body was, nothing between me and bare sky. How little heat was there left in the sun – what did I want?

*To kiss you and die.*

The next morning, in the library, by chance, looking for something to comfort me, I took down a volume of Bach cantatas. *Ich habe genug.* Yes. That's what I felt, this is enough, and has at the same moment no hope, no other thing, no else.

*I have seen you. You fill my eyes.*

# Snow White & Rose Red

*You do not know you've been forgiven.*
Anna Akhmatova, "Sweetbriar in Blossom"

### (i) Veil

*Hark!* says the baby.

Warm air passes through this baking attic from the curved, open window.
Maple leaves. The friendliness of tree.

*Listen,* it says. *I am walking in a white sand place.*
*I am running down there in the secret dunes of your sand hills.*

There are white sheets on the bed, white pillow cases, the duvet uncovered.
Faint, tea-coloured cotton. The sheets are old. They would have wrapped this
one if she had been born.

I cannot look at things, at formed, present things.

I have pinned up a white translucent scarf in the alcove, so that it falls
from the sloped attic ceiling to the floor at the foot of my bed. Air from the
window wafts this veil that hangs between me and what I am unable to look
at.

I lie still while the next pain wave passes. My body tries to expel the tissue
that is left. I can bear the fullness, the heat, the sweating, when I am alone
like this.

*Don't leave me.*

I can bear the animal *No* that my body has said to me.

It is a live knowing.
I listen.
I do what it says.

## (ii) White Camel

*Two things helped –*
*the second arriving long after the first,*
*which was now, in the room.*

A child's cut-out, a little camel made of foam core, which he gave her
after he had finished making the other puppets –
just shapes, really – but she wanted the white camel.

When the time came
she put a rope of beads around the camel's neck
so the never-to-be, the not-born,
could play with it.
And she stood the little camel under the skylight
in the attic room.

She covered everything in white.
By the time he arrived,
there was no place for him: nowhere to read the newspaper,
to put his wallet down, or his keys, the change
from his pockets.

Even the harpsichord in the corner, closed
and shrouded. The table with its unbleached cloth, placemats
she had made from the torn pillow cases. And her dishes,
made of that hard French glass, had always unnerved him,
especially now – he could not bear any aspect of her
to be transparent, as the child seemed to be, to her,
as she had said it was, for the instant that it was – alive.

She, wanting only to lie on those faint, soft sheets, behind
that muslin veil, must have taken the small translucent sac,
there, in her hand – *something like sea water,*

*something inside it – clear,* so she could see through,
*and inside that, something else –* must have carried it with her,
in the taxi, all the way to the hospital.
Wanting what was not to be so.


By the time he arrived,
there was nothing left for him to do.


Here, in this fresh breeze
that flows over the shaded bed, he wants
to lift her up out of her private grief
that excludes him, but his relief
that there is no child runs
from the pores of his skin like an oil
he knows she can smell.

He lies down
beside her. And she lies – at first
facing away from him – then turns,
leaning up on her elbow,
addresses him, and begins to speak.
He listens as if the story doesn't belong to him –
listens (it will startle him)
as long as she continues telling it
to the skylight, the attic walls, the camel
with its bead necklace – long after
he collects himself, descends
into the street by the outside stairs, finds
himself in his car (he recognizes the camel's beads –
she must have taken them from his store of props –
pearls, made of paste), winding through the market,
out onto the drive, past the art gallery,

the tight lawns, the intense congealed summer
that the city makes.

                    It will startle him
that she wanted this so much.


When she next comes to visit, he will build her a pyre
by the barbeque in his back field where she can lay
the little boxes she has been hoarding –

inside, the colour of apricots, outside,
a shimmer of writing in silver.

In each one,
an egg shell, broken open.

She saves the shells and washes them, puts
one half back inside the other.

                Alone in the car, he imagines her, like someone
                crossing a desert,
                threading along with the camel –

                he sees how small the camel is, he sees how small
                their not-child is, sees
                how the camel carries this small thing
                perfectly.


                She
                watches through the sloping skylight, tells
                the lost child everything she
                remembers of its time with her,
                weeps and weeps –

but not for no one,
or no thing.


*Here is your tiny camel –*
*little things I saved for you.*
*White beads, some leaves*
*from spring, in frost –*
*white blades from grass.*
*(Small grub. White spring.)*

*Here is the rock I named for you,*
*the stone I laid and breathed into –*
*let be, smallest one, and if*
*you can't be formed,*
*don't come.*

*(This was the song I sang for you.)*


Beyond the sweltering city, he notices
a change in the sky.

### (iii) A Day for the Heroes

*Now the thorns on this rose are its teeth,* she
tells him. (She tells him nothing – she will
bring him close, never exactly, not quite there.)

She winds it back from the ending, floating
out as close to the beginning
as she can get.

This one: that she walked straight up the outside stairs to the attic apartment
on a late March day, with everything swollen, especially her ankles, especially
the bushes in the side yard, their stems yellow, only the roots showing red, the
ground all raw around them, and she thought, *I belong now. To it.*

Another one, for him: the long unpronounceable German expression he said
to her that morning as she lay over the car's hood, just for joy – the perfect
day, early March, and snow like crystal on the new grass blades – a sudden
springing up inside her.

> *Es ist ein Tag um Helden zu zeugen,*
> then cleared his throat,
> *a day for the – how do you say it –*
> *for the  – insemination of heroes.*

> She laughed and laughed.

> *Well it is said like that,* he said, *this was*
> *an old expression of my mother's – but*
> *what they mean by it –*

> *They mean, to make heroes,* she said to him.

*They mean it is a day of days, for holy love.*

*A day for the gods,* she said.

And he said, *To do what they like with us.*

## (iv) Song for the Bear

All winter, it was like an old fairy tale, the way
she came and went. In real life, their roles reversed:
he who kept the hearth, she who appeared
in the cold. He who provided the warmth
of his body, his coat, his heart – completely
misunderstanding that inside her was the possibility,
probability now, of a birth and a being
half-him, half-her – magic enough
in any time.

                                    All winter
she was content to sing along with him,
meeting at the hearthstone, in the heat
of that fire. But by early spring
something changed in her, and the night she came,
late, in the fog, half distracted from wanting,
waiting, for him to say he would acknowledge it –
late, confused, and in tears – they held together
under the covers and, for that instant,
she wished it dead.

> *If I came to your door, in a cloak,* she said,
> *lost, abandoned, cast out –a child, not yours,*
> *in my belly, you'd take me in –* struggling through snow,
> wound round in the storm wraith –
> *raise it as your own. Yes I would,*
> he said, *yes. But it is mine,*
> *and I am afraid.*

## (v) Rose Red

*She will bring him close. Never*
*exactly, not quite near – until,*
*a long time after, the second thing appears.*


There is a place where the rock has split –
a bush grows out of it. There are two ways
you can go there:


The first is public, anyone might find it. Take the track in from the Sable
Road to Craig's Beach, continue on by the edge of the marsh until you
come to the creek's mouth. Follow the brackish water out to sea and
look for the cormorants on the big square rock. Now you have lost sight
of the true destination – passed it by.


For the other way, one has to know the path,
though random travelling might give up
the secret. This is a true geography,
and you are put on notice
not to use this map.


After you have traversed the salt marsh, from the east, cross the creek,
then follow the shore a ways. When you come to a little sand beach
clearly visible at low tide, just past the long shoulder of beach rocks,
walk on staying close to the shore until you come to a high big rock.
Climb up – on the top you will see quartz striations roughly in the
shape of a cross,  running north and south, east and west. Look for an
opening through the alders and bayberry, and enter the clearing that
contains two sweetbriar rose bushes.

The land dips down suddenly –
You will be in one of the old dunes
of the Sand Hills.


This is not the place – it is like the place, but if you manage to arrive here you
will have understood the territory. Even if you thought you knew exactly, you
would be sure to lose your way. These places are protected.


*The thorns on this rose are its teeth,*
she tells him.


The sweetbriar is an old bush – its branches, leaves, and blossoms smell
like apples mixed with roses. Even in winter there is a faint scent. This
sweetbriar is so old its branches fall down around its feet like hair.


*Come into this place where the rock has split –*
*the bush grows out of it,*
*you will recognize its smell.*


The rose stretches out, branches pushing up
against the spruce that grow above it.
Below, a simple mound, outline of stone,
the ancient cellar-hole filled in by time – increment
of leaf, mould, needles from the spruce
and nearby fir, flecks ground up from rock,
particles of shell, green spines from the sea urchin.

*This is sand,* she tells the baby.

By weight of water –

*This is rain.*

Inside the cleft, a shoot, arterial,
comes now, this June day –
out of the brown needles, the rock's hidden room –

so red, shot from the rose,
thrusting straight up towards the dark overgrowth.

It will die, looking for light.

*It will not die.*

She cuts away the tensile spruce,
the pink-cored limbs
that threaten now to suck the sun
and kill the rose –

she scrapes the cuttings clean,
the branches bleed their balsam balm
to seal the openings shut.

*The wound is closed, and nothing more will grow.*

The rose helps her – and
she helps the rose.

Perfect fingernail of thorn –
each one intact,
curled into itself – protects
the still furled flame.

ζ

# Arioso

Then the voice will come and fill up the spaces in the violins. The scraped bellies of the cellos will fill, and the violas, the double basses the size of children, each one holding a voice. And that voice will mount up, will press into the spaces between things, the layers of socks, folded, of woollen shirts in bureau drawers, of empty coat sleeves, hats without heads. It will press between the edges of bricks, the tails of rats lying close in a cold wind, it will wind into the backs of clouds – it will howl, it will enter every bowl that has ever held soup, it will sing for its supper, it will sup. It will whine and then plead, it will soften and then it will ask –

*Are you warm enough? Have you light? Are you cold? Would you like something to eat? Is there someone with you? Are you alone?*

And then you will cry and lie down in your feather bed and feel the great skims of your loneliness lifting away from you. Someone will speak to you and a change come over you, your skin will be moist and fresh and remember itself, its own name. Then the winnowing will come through you and you will sit up, and laugh, and go out under the trees, and a coil unwind in your throat, and the arc of your singing will come out.

## Notes and Sources

"Boat" is for Veryan Haysom.

"Last Summer in the Old Craig House" is for my sister, Cindy Pierce Embree.

"A girl awake"
The ell of a house refers to an extension of a building, usually built at right angles. Here, the ell-chamber was a tiny room off an upstairs bedroom over the kitchen in the ell of an old Cape Cod style house.

"Aunt Edna" is for Edna Bain Lloyd (Mrs. Percy Mouzar), *in memoriam* (1906-1992), and for Babo Kamel.

"Their Boy" is for Jeremy McKenna Harris, *in memoriam* (1980-2005).

"Common Loons" is for Catherine McClearn Pross.

"*Vox humana*": an organ reed stop which produces tones imitative of the human voice.

"*Vox animalia*" is for Jan Curtis.

"My Jerusalem" is for Liliana Kleiner.

"You wrote to me" is for George Steeves.

"Madonna of the Pinks" is for Barry Dempster.

"The Returning" is for Dayne Ogilvie (1950-2006) and for Laura Gainey (1981-2006), *in memoriam*. On the night of December 8, 2006, while I was writing the poem for Dayne who had died six weeks earlier at Pleasant Point, Shelburne County, the news came over CBC radio that Laura Gainey had been swept overboard in a storm from the tall ship, Picton Castle, out of Lunenburg, NS.

"Penthesilea's Horse" is for Cynthia French.

"Cio-Cio San Arrives at Your Door" is for Janet Barkhouse, and for Kate Krug whose portrait it turned out to be.

"Athena's Hand on Cassandra's Shoulder" is for Eleanor Wilner.

"Anastasia's Soldier" is for Marianne Bochdanetzky, *in memoriam.*

"Sestina on Six Words from Frances Itani's *Deafening*"
Brief quotations from *Deafening* by Frances Itani (Harper Flamingo, 2003) are noted in italics throughout the poem.

"*Ich habe genug*: It Is Enough" is for Dayne Ogilvie and Gary Akenhead.

"Arioso": Italian "airy," a musical term which describes a state of singing between recitative and aria, between speech rhythm and song; also a movement in some Baroque compositions.

≈

The Jeremy Harris Living Library at L'Arche Cape Breton: www.larchecapebreton.org

The Dayne Ogilvie Grant for an Emerging Gay Writer, The Writers' Trust of Canada: www.writerstrust.com

The Gainey Foundation: www.gaineyfoundation.com

# Acknowledgements

A number of the poems in *Vox Humana* first appeared in literary publications, often in different forms and sometimes under other titles. My thanks to the editors of these publications, and to the judges of competitions who first gave them their attention: *The Fiddlehead, Contemporary Verse 2, The New Quarterly, Vintage 97-98, Arc, The English Journal,* and *The Literary Review of Canada (LRC).*

"Sestina on Six Words from Frances Itani's *Deafening*" was commissioned by CBC Radio One (Sydney, NS) for "Ask the Poets" in conjunction with Canada Reads, 2006. Other work was broadcast on CBC Radio Two (Halifax) on the occasion of the Nova Scotia Talent Trust's 60th Anniversary Gala.

"Common Loons" placed third in *Arc's* Poem of the Year competition, 2009, and "Snow White & Rose Red" was short-listed for The CBC Literary Awards. "Shelter" won *The Fiddlehead* Poetry Prize before it was re-named the Ralph Gustafson Award.

Other poems have been anthologized in *Words Out There: Women Poets in Atlantic Canada,* edited by Jeanette Lynes (Roseway); *The Hoodoo You Do So Well: Poetry From The Banff Centre Writing Studio* (littlefishcartpress); and *Undercurrents: New Voices in Canadian Poetry,* edited by Robyn Sarah (Cormorant).

The friends and supporters of this book are many. I want to acknowledge first my editor, Barry Dempster for his steadfast, insightful attention – inspired editing from the heart and soul of a major poet.

I have been fortunate in my early readers: Don McKay has been part of the book's development from its beginnings in an early manuscript; Eleanor Wilner, Heather McHugh, Renate Wood, and Carl Phillips read and influenced my earlier work at Warren Wilson's MFA Program for Writers;

my alumnae colleagues from Warren Wilson, notably Carolyn West and Babo Kamel, and my manuscript review cohorts Anne Sullivan, Susan Sindall, and Wendy Hawken, each made valuable contributions.

My grateful thanks to others who have read my work at various points along the way: Sue Chenette, Lorri Neilsen Glenn, Don Hannah, Catherine Joyce, Basma Kavanagh, Fiona Lam, Daphne Marlatt, Teresa O'Brien, Elizabeth Phillips, Robyn Sarah, Jan Zwicky; and my colleagues at Cape Breton University, Jan Curtis, Jane Farnsworth, and John Lingard. At the Banff Centre, Stephanie Bolster and John Glenday contributed to the work at a much later stage.

For ongoing support in ways both concrete and spiritual: Kim Atwood, Colin Bernhardt, Don Hannah & Doug Guildford, Prune Harris, Afra Kavanagh, Marilyn O'Neil, Marjorie Skott, Gillian Thomas & Donna E. Smyth.

Thank you to my benefactors for the gift of time that has allowed me to write: Gary Akenhead, Babo & Orin Edwards, Cynthia & Les French, Laine Gifford & Jonathan Roosevelt, Timothy Gillespie, Linda Moore, Sue Roberts, Nancy & Ron Roth.

Thanks to Ruth Roach Pierson and Gudrun & Heinrich Pelkner for their help with the German in the book – any remaining inaccuracies belong to me and to the poems.

To the production team at Brick, my heartfelt thanks to Alayna Munce for her inspired editing and steadfast care and concern, to Cheryl Dipede and Alan & Rita Siu for their meticulous care in every detail, and to Kitty Lewis for her unfailing enthusiasm, her intuitive understanding of the writer's needs and those of the book.

For artistic and financial support: The Banff Centre, The Canada Council for the Arts, The Nova Scotia Department of Culture, and The Nova Scotia Talent Trust.

To my Sable River community of friends and family, and to the Doo, my thanks for accepting the ways of a writer, for knowing when to come to the door and when to stay away.

To my ongoing poetry group, Cynthia French, Jan Barkhouse, and Veryan Haysom, my thanks for being my inspiration, my fiercest critics, the friends of my poems.

To Kate Krug, for arriving in the very nick of time, and for her fine work on the copy edits, my admiration, love, and gratitude.

## Biographical Note

E. Alex Pierce lives in East Sable River, Nova Scotia where she is developing a centre for writers and artists. In her earlier life she taught voice, movement, and mask for the theatre, and created original collaborative works with visual artists and composers. For ten years she taught creative writing (playwriting and poetry) at Cape Breton University, and is currently Series Editor for the CBU Press publication,  *The Essential Cape Breton Library.* She holds a Master of Fine Arts in Creative Writing from Warren Wilson College, and has twice been a participant in the Writing Studio at the Banff Centre. Her work has been anthologized in *Words Out There: Women Poets in Atlantic Canada* (Roseway); *Best Canadian Poetry 2008* (Tightrope); and in *Undercurrents: New Voices in Canadian Poetry* (Cormorant).